# 50 The Best Italian Dessert Recipes

By: Kelly Johnson

# Table of Contents

- Tiramisu
- Cannoli
- Panna Cotta
- Ricotta Cheesecake
- Zabaione
- Sfogliatella
- Biscotti
- Cantucci
- Italian Ricotta Pie
- Cassata
- Baba au Rhum
- Semifreddo
- Budino
- Torta della Nonna
- Bomboloni
- Amaretti Cookies
- Crostata
- Panforte
- Granita
- Gelato
- Affogato
- Zeppole
- Strudel
- Sfinci
- Frittelle
- Torta Caprese
- Pastiera Napoletana
- Mont Blanc
- Maritozzi
- Ricciarelli
- Crespelle
- Torta di Mele (Apple Cake)
- Pasticciotto
- Sfogliatine
- Arancini di Riso (Rice Balls)
- Gattò di Patate (Potato Cake)

- Salame di Cioccolato
- Biancomangiare
- Panettone
- Colomba Pasquale
- Ricotta and Pear Tart
- Focaccia Dolce
- Zuppa Inglese
- Castagnaccio
- Tortino al Cioccolato
- Sbrisolona
- Pasticcini alla Crema
- Focaccia di Recco
- Ciambellone
- Frutta Martorana

## Tiramisu

**Ingredients:**

- 1 cup **heavy cream**
- 1/2 cup **sugar**
- 1 cup **mascarpone cheese**
- 1 cup **strong coffee (cooled)**
- 1 tbsp **dark rum** (optional)
- **Ladyfingers**
- **Cocoa powder for dusting**

**Instructions:**

1. Whip cream and sugar until soft peaks form.
2. Fold mascarpone cheese into whipped cream until smooth.
3. Mix coffee and rum, then dip ladyfingers quickly into the mixture.
4. Layer soaked ladyfingers and mascarpone mixture in a dish.
5. Repeat layers, then chill for 4–6 hours.
6. Dust with cocoa powder before serving.

## Cannoli

**Ingredients:**

- **Shells:** 1 1/2 cups **flour**, 2 tbsp **sugar**, 1/2 tsp **cinnamon**, 1 tbsp **unsalted butter**, 1/4 cup **red wine**
- **Filling:** 1 1/2 cups **ricotta cheese**, 1/2 cup **powdered sugar**, 1/4 tsp **vanilla extract**, **chocolate chips (optional)**

**Instructions:**

1. Mix flour, sugar, cinnamon, and butter, then slowly add wine to form a dough.
2. Roll dough thin, cut into circles, and wrap around cannoli tubes.
3. Fry in hot oil until golden, then cool.
4. Mix ricotta, powdered sugar, and vanilla for filling.
5. Pipe filling into cooled shells and sprinkle with chocolate chips or pistachios.

## Panna Cotta

**Ingredients:**

- 2 cups **heavy cream**
- 1/4 cup **sugar**
- 1 tsp **vanilla extract**
- 1 tsp **gelatin powder**
- 2 tbsp **water**

**Instructions:**

1. Dissolve gelatin in cold water.
2. Heat cream and sugar in a saucepan until the sugar dissolves.
3. Stir in gelatin and vanilla extract.
4. Pour into ramekins and refrigerate for 4 hours or until set.
5. Serve with fruit, caramel, or chocolate sauce.

## Ricotta Cheesecake

**Ingredients:**

- 2 cups **ricotta cheese**
- 1/2 cup **cream cheese**
- 1 cup **sugar**
- 3 **eggs**
- 1 tsp **vanilla extract**
- 1/4 cup **heavy cream**
- **Graham cracker crust**

**Instructions:**

1. Preheat the oven to 325°F (165°C).
2. Blend ricotta, cream cheese, sugar, eggs, vanilla, and cream until smooth.
3. Pour into a graham cracker crust and bake for 50 minutes.
4. Let cool and refrigerate for at least 4 hours before serving.

## Zabaione

### Ingredients:

- 6 **egg yolks**
- 1/2 cup **sugar**
- 1 cup **Marsala wine** (or other sweet wine)

### Instructions:

1. Whisk egg yolks and sugar in a bowl.
2. Heat wine in a double boiler and slowly add to the egg mixture while whisking continuously.
3. Continue whisking until the mixture thickens and becomes frothy.
4. Serve warm or chilled.

## Sfogliatella

### Ingredients:

- 2 cups **flour**
- 1/4 cup **sugar**
- 1/2 tsp **salt**
- 1/4 cup **unsalted butter**, softened
- 1/2 cup **water**
- **Filling:** 1 1/2 cups **ricotta cheese**, 1/4 cup **candied orange peel**, 1/4 tsp **cinnamon**, 1/4 cup **sugar**

### Instructions:

1. Mix flour, sugar, and salt, then cut in butter until crumbly.
2. Gradually add water to form a dough and let rest.
3. For the filling, combine ricotta, candied orange peel, cinnamon, and sugar.
4. Roll out dough and fill with ricotta mixture.
5. Fold into a shell and bake at 375°F (190°C) for 30 minutes.

## Biscotti

### Ingredients:

- 2 cups **flour**
- 1 cup **sugar**
- 1 tsp **baking powder**
- 2 **eggs**
- 1 tsp **vanilla extract**
- 1/2 cup **almonds (optional)**

### Instructions:

1. Preheat oven to 350°F (175°C).
2. Mix flour, sugar, baking powder, eggs, and vanilla until a dough forms.
3. Fold in almonds if desired.
4. Shape into a log and bake for 25 minutes.
5. Slice and bake again for 10 minutes until crisp.

## Cantucci

**Ingredients:**

- 2 cups **flour**
- 1 cup **sugar**
- 1/2 tsp **baking powder**
- 2 **eggs**
- 1 tsp **vanilla extract**
- 1/2 cup **hazelnuts (or almonds)**

**Instructions:**

1. Preheat oven to 350°F (175°C).
2. Mix flour, sugar, baking powder, eggs, and vanilla to form a dough.
3. Fold in nuts.
4. Shape into a log, bake for 20 minutes, then slice and bake for 10 minutes until crisp.

## Italian Ricotta Pie

### Ingredients:

- 2 cups **ricotta cheese**
- 1 cup **sugar**
- 3 **eggs**
- 1/2 tsp **vanilla extract**
- 1/4 tsp **cinnamon**
- **Pie crust**

### Instructions:

1. Preheat oven to 350°F (175°C).
2. Mix ricotta, sugar, eggs, vanilla, and cinnamon until smooth.
3. Pour into pie crust and bake for 45–50 minutes until set.
4. Let cool before serving.

## Cassata

**Ingredients:**

- 2 cups **ricotta cheese**
- 1/2 cup **sugar**
- 1/4 cup **candied fruit**
- 1 cup **chocolate chips**
- **Sponge cake layers**

**Instructions:**

1. Mix ricotta and sugar until smooth, then fold in fruit and chocolate chips.
2. Layer ricotta mixture between sponge cake layers.
3. Refrigerate for a few hours before serving.

## Baba au Rhum

### Ingredients:

- 1 1/2 cups **flour**
- 1/4 cup **sugar**
- 1/2 tsp **instant yeast**
- 1/4 cup **milk**
- 2 **eggs**
- 1/4 cup **rum**
- **Syrup**: 1 cup **water**, 1/2 cup **sugar**, 1/2 cup **rum**

### Instructions:

1. Mix flour, sugar, yeast, milk, and eggs to form a dough.
2. Let rise, then shape into small balls.
3. Bake at 375°F (190°C) for 20 minutes.
4. Soak in rum syrup for 10 minutes before serving.

## Semifreddo

### Ingredients:

- 1 cup **heavy cream**
- 1/2 cup **sugar**
- 3 **egg yolks**
- 1 tsp **vanilla extract**
- 1/2 cup **mascarpone cheese**
- 2 tbsp **dark chocolate (optional)**

### Instructions:

1. Whip heavy cream until stiff peaks form and set aside.
2. Whisk egg yolks and sugar until pale and fluffy.
3. Gently fold mascarpone into the egg mixture, then fold in whipped cream.
4. Add chocolate if using and mix lightly.
5. Pour into a loaf pan and freeze for at least 6 hours before serving.

## Budino

### Ingredients:

- 2 cups **milk**
- 1/2 cup **sugar**
- 1/4 cup **cornstarch**
- 1 tsp **vanilla extract**
- 1/4 cup **dark chocolate** (optional)

### Instructions:

1. Heat milk and sugar in a saucepan over medium heat.
2. Whisk cornstarch into a little cold milk, then add to the hot milk mixture.
3. Stir constantly until it thickens, then remove from heat and add vanilla.
4. Pour into cups and let cool before refrigerating for 2–3 hours.
5. Top with melted chocolate if desired.

## Torta della Nonna

**Ingredients:**

- **Pastry Cream:** 1 cup **milk**, 1/4 cup **sugar**, 2 **egg yolks**, 1 tbsp **cornstarch**, 1 tsp **vanilla extract**
- **Crust:** 2 cups **flour**, 1/2 cup **sugar**, 1/2 cup **butter**, 1 **egg**

**Instructions:**

1. For the crust, mix flour, sugar, butter, and egg into a dough, then chill for 30 minutes.
2. For the pastry cream, heat milk and sugar in a saucepan. Whisk egg yolks and cornstarch, then pour into hot milk mixture.
3. Cook until thickened, then stir in vanilla and cool.
4. Roll out the dough and line a tart pan. Fill with pastry cream and top with dough strips.
5. Bake at 350°F (175°C) for 30–40 minutes.

## Bomboloni

### Ingredients:

- 2 1/2 cups **flour**
- 1/4 cup **sugar**
- 1 tsp **instant yeast**
- 1/2 cup **milk**
- 2 **eggs**
- **Filling:** 1/2 cup **Nutella** or **custard**
- **Powdered sugar for dusting**

### Instructions:

1. Mix flour, sugar, and yeast, then add eggs and warm milk to form a dough.
2. Let dough rise for 1–2 hours.
3. Shape into balls and deep-fry until golden.
4. Fill with Nutella or custard, then dust with powdered sugar.

## Amaretti Cookies

**Ingredients:**

- 1 1/2 cups **almond flour**
- 1 cup **sugar**
- 2 **egg whites**
- 1 tsp **almond extract**
- **Powdered sugar for dusting**

**Instructions:**

1. Preheat oven to 325°F (165°C).
2. Whip egg whites until stiff peaks form, then fold in sugar, almond flour, and almond extract.
3. Shape into small balls and place on a baking sheet.
4. Dust with powdered sugar and bake for 15–20 minutes.

## Crostata

**Ingredients:**

- **Crust:** 2 cups **flour**, 1/2 cup **sugar**, 1/2 cup **butter**, 1 **egg**
- **Filling:** 1 1/2 cups **fruit preserves** (apricot, raspberry, etc.)

**Instructions:**

1. Mix flour, sugar, butter, and egg to form dough. Chill for 30 minutes.
2. Roll out dough and line a tart pan, then spread fruit preserves.
3. Roll out the remaining dough for the lattice top.
4. Bake at 375°F (190°C) for 30–40 minutes.

## Panforte

**Ingredients:**

- 1 1/2 cups **hazelnuts, almonds,** and **walnuts** (chopped)
- 1 cup **dried fruit** (raisins, figs)
- 1/2 cup **honey**
- 1/2 cup **sugar**
- 1 tsp **cinnamon, cloves,** and **nutmeg**
- 1/4 cup **flour**
- 2 tbsp **cocoa powder**
- 1/4 tsp **baking soda**

**Instructions:**

1. Preheat oven to 325°F (165°C).
2. Toast nuts and fruit in a pan, then mix with spices, flour, cocoa, and baking soda.
3. Heat honey and sugar in a saucepan until the sugar dissolves.
4. Combine with dry ingredients and bake for 30 minutes.
5. Let cool and slice.

## Granita

**Ingredients:**

- 2 cups **water**
- 1 cup **sugar**
- 2 cups **fruit juice** (lemon, strawberry, or peach)

**Instructions:**

1. Boil water and sugar until the sugar dissolves.
2. Stir in fruit juice and refrigerate.
3. Every 30 minutes, scrape the mixture with a fork to form crystals.
4. Serve chilled.

## Gelato

**Ingredients:**

- 2 cups **milk**
- 1 cup **heavy cream**
- 3/4 cup **sugar**
- 4 **egg yolks**
- 1 tsp **vanilla extract**

**Instructions:**

1. Heat milk and cream in a saucepan.
2. Whisk egg yolks and sugar, then pour in hot milk mixture.
3. Cook until it thickens.
4. Chill the mixture, then churn in an ice cream maker until smooth.

## Affogato

### Ingredients:

- 2 scoops **vanilla gelato**
- 1 shot **hot espresso**

### Instructions:

1. Place gelato in a glass or bowl.
2. Pour hot espresso over the gelato.
3. Serve immediately.

## Zeppole

**Ingredients:**

- 2 cups **flour**
- 1/2 cup **water**
- 1/2 cup **sugar**
- 1 tsp **baking powder**
- 2 **eggs**
- **Filling:** 1/2 cup **custard** or **ricotta**
- **Powdered sugar for dusting**

**Instructions:**

1. Mix flour, water, sugar, baking powder, and eggs into a dough.
2. Fry spoonfuls of dough in hot oil until golden.
3. Fill with custard or ricotta, then dust with powdered sugar.

## Strudel

**Ingredients:**

- **Filling:** 4 cups **apples** (peeled, cored, and sliced), 1/2 cup **sugar**, 1/2 tsp **cinnamon**, 1/4 cup **raisins** (optional), 1/4 cup **chopped walnuts** (optional)
- 1 package **phyllo dough**
- 1/4 cup **butter**, melted
- **Powdered sugar for dusting**

**Instructions:**

1. Preheat the oven to 375°F (190°C).
2. Toss apple slices with sugar, cinnamon, raisins, and walnuts.
3. Lay a sheet of phyllo dough on a clean surface, brush with butter, and layer 3 more sheets.
4. Spread the apple mixture on the dough and roll it up.
5. Place on a baking sheet, brush with butter, and bake for 30–40 minutes.
6. Dust with powdered sugar before serving.

## Sfinci

### Ingredients:

- 2 cups **flour**
- 1 tbsp **sugar**
- 2 tsp **baking powder**
- 1/2 tsp **salt**
- 2 **eggs**
- 1/2 cup **water**
- **Powdered sugar for dusting**
- **Honey for drizzling**

### Instructions:

1. Mix flour, sugar, baking powder, and salt.
2. Add eggs and water, mixing to form a dough.
3. Heat oil in a frying pan and drop spoonfuls of dough into the hot oil.
4. Fry until golden and drain on paper towels.
5. Drizzle with honey and dust with powdered sugar.

## Frittelle

**Ingredients:**

- 2 cups **flour**
- 1/2 cup **sugar**
- 1 tsp **baking powder**
- 2 **eggs**
- 1/4 cup **milk**
- 1/2 tsp **vanilla extract**
- **Powdered sugar for dusting**

**Instructions:**

1. Mix flour, sugar, and baking powder.
2. Whisk eggs, milk, and vanilla, then combine with dry ingredients to form a batter.
3. Heat oil in a frying pan and drop spoonfuls of batter into the hot oil.
4. Fry until golden, then drain on paper towels.
5. Dust with powdered sugar.

## Torta Caprese

**Ingredients:**

- 1 1/2 cups **almond flour**
- 1/2 cup **sugar**
- 1/4 cup **unsweetened cocoa powder**
- 1/4 tsp **baking powder**
- 3 **eggs**
- 1/2 cup **butter**, melted
- 1/2 tsp **vanilla extract**
- **Powdered sugar for dusting**

**Instructions:**

1. Preheat the oven to 350°F (175°C).
2. Mix almond flour, sugar, cocoa powder, and baking powder in a bowl.
3. Beat eggs, then add melted butter and vanilla.
4. Combine with dry ingredients and pour into a greased pan.
5. Bake for 25–30 minutes, then let cool.
6. Dust with powdered sugar before serving.

## Pastiera Napoletana

### Ingredients:

- **Crust:** 2 cups **flour**, 1/2 cup **butter**, 1/4 cup **sugar**, 1 **egg**
- **Filling:** 1 1/2 cups **cooked wheat berries**, 1 cup **ricotta cheese**, 1/2 cup **sugar**, 3 **eggs**, 1 tsp **orange blossom water**, 1 tsp **cinnamon**, 1/2 cup **candied fruit** (optional)

### Instructions:

1. For the crust, mix flour, butter, sugar, and egg to form a dough. Chill for 30 minutes.
2. For the filling, mix cooked wheat berries, ricotta, sugar, eggs, orange blossom water, and cinnamon.
3. Roll out dough and line a pie dish, then pour in the filling.
4. Bake at 350°F (175°C) for 45 minutes, then let cool.

## Mont Blanc

**Ingredients:**

- 2 cups **chestnut puree**
- 1/2 cup **whipped cream**
- 1/4 cup **sugar**
- 1/4 tsp **vanilla extract**
- **Meringue bases** (optional)

**Instructions:**

1. Whip cream with sugar and vanilla until soft peaks form.
2. Pipe chestnut puree onto meringue bases, if using.
3. Top with whipped cream and garnish with chestnut pieces or chocolate.

## Maritozzi

### Ingredients:

- 3 cups **flour**
- 1/2 cup **sugar**
- 2 tsp **instant yeast**
- 1/2 cup **milk**, warm
- 2 **eggs**
- 1/2 cup **butter**, softened
- **Whipped cream for filling**

### Instructions:

1. Mix flour, sugar, and yeast, then add warm milk, eggs, and butter.
2. Knead the dough until smooth, then let rise for 1–2 hours.
3. Shape into buns and bake at 350°F (175°C) for 20 minutes.
4. Once cooled, slice and fill with whipped cream.

## Ricciarelli

**Ingredients:**

- 1 1/2 cups **almond flour**
- 1 cup **powdered sugar**
- 2 **egg whites**
- 1 tsp **vanilla extract**
- **Powdered sugar for dusting**

**Instructions:**

1. Preheat oven to 350°F (175°C).
2. Whisk egg whites until stiff peaks form.
3. Fold in almond flour, powdered sugar, and vanilla.
4. Shape into small ovals and place on a baking sheet.
5. Bake for 10–12 minutes, then dust with powdered sugar.

## Crespelle

### Ingredients:

- 1 cup **flour**
- 1 cup **milk**
- 2 **eggs**
- 1 tbsp **butter**
- **Filling:** 1/2 cup **ricotta cheese**, 1/2 cup **spinach**, 1/4 cup **parmesan cheese**

### Instructions:

1. Whisk flour, milk, eggs, and butter to form a batter.
2. Pour batter into a hot pan and cook thin crepes.
3. For filling, mix ricotta, spinach, and parmesan.
4. Fill the crepes with ricotta mixture, roll up, and bake at 350°F (175°C) for 15 minutes.

## Torta di Mele (Apple Cake)

**Ingredients:**

- 2 cups **flour**
- 1 cup **sugar**
- 2 **eggs**
- 1/2 cup **butter**, softened
- 1/2 cup **milk**
- 3 **apples**, peeled and sliced
- 1 tsp **baking powder**
- 1 tsp **cinnamon**

**Instructions:**

1. Preheat oven to 350°F (175°C).
2. Mix flour, sugar, baking powder, and cinnamon.
3. Beat eggs, then add butter and milk.
4. Fold in dry ingredients and apples.
5. Pour into a greased pan and bake for 35–40 minutes until golden.

## Pasticciotto

### Ingredients:

- **Dough:** 2 1/2 cups **flour**, 1/2 cup **sugar**, 1/2 cup **butter**, 1 **egg**, 1 tsp **vanilla extract**, 1/4 cup **milk**
- **Filling:** 1 cup **pastry cream** (made with 2 cups milk, 1/2 cup sugar, 2 egg yolks, 2 tbsp cornstarch)

### Instructions:

1. Preheat oven to 350°F (175°C).
2. Mix flour, sugar, butter, egg, vanilla, and milk to form a dough.
3. Roll out the dough and line individual tart molds.
4. Fill with pastry cream.
5. Cover with more dough, sealing the edges, and bake for 20–25 minutes until golden.

## Sfogliatine

**Ingredients:**

- 1 sheet **puff pastry**
- 1/2 cup **pastry cream** or **whipped cream**
- **Powdered sugar for dusting**

**Instructions:**

1. Preheat the oven to 400°F (200°C).
2. Roll out puff pastry and cut into rectangles.
3. Bake for 10-12 minutes until puffed and golden.
4. Once cooled, slice in half horizontally and fill with pastry cream or whipped cream.
5. Dust with powdered sugar.

## Arancini di Riso (Rice Balls)

### Ingredients:

- 2 cups **cooked risotto rice** (preferably cold)
- 1/2 cup **parmesan cheese**, grated
- 1/4 cup **peas**, cooked
- 1/2 cup **mozzarella**, diced
- 2 **eggs**
- 1/2 cup **flour**
- 1 1/2 cups **bread crumbs**
- **Oil for frying**

### Instructions:

1. Mix cooled risotto rice, parmesan, peas, and mozzarella.
2. Shape into small balls, then dip in flour, beaten eggs, and breadcrumbs.
3. Heat oil in a pan and fry the rice balls until golden and crispy.
4. Drain on paper towels and serve hot.

## Gattò di Patate (Potato Cake)

**Ingredients:**

- 2 lbs **potatoes**, peeled and boiled
- 1/2 cup **butter**
- 1/2 cup **milk**
- 1 cup **parmesan cheese**, grated
- 2 **eggs**
- 1/2 cup **mozzarella cheese**, cubed
- **Salt and pepper** to taste
- 1/2 cup **bread crumbs**

**Instructions:**

1. Preheat the oven to 375°F (190°C).
2. Mash the boiled potatoes and mix with butter, milk, parmesan, eggs, mozzarella, salt, and pepper.
3. Pour into a greased baking dish, sprinkle with breadcrumbs, and bake for 25–30 minutes until golden.

## Salame di Cioccolato (Chocolate Salami)

### Ingredients:

- 200g **dark chocolate**
- 100g **butter**
- 1/2 cup **sugar**
- 1 tbsp **rum**
- 2 cups **biscuit crumbs** (or crushed cookies)
- **Powdered sugar for dusting**

### Instructions:

1. Melt chocolate and butter over low heat.
2. Stir in sugar and rum, then add biscuit crumbs.
3. Roll the mixture into a log shape and refrigerate for 2 hours.
4. Dust with powdered sugar before slicing.

## Biancomangiare

### Ingredients:

- 2 cups **milk**
- 1/2 cup **sugar**
- 2 tbsp **cornstarch**
- 1 tsp **vanilla extract**
- **Slivered almonds for garnish**

### Instructions:

1. Heat milk and sugar in a saucepan.
2. Mix cornstarch with a little cold milk, then add to the hot milk mixture.
3. Stir until thickened, then remove from heat and add vanilla extract.
4. Pour into molds and refrigerate until set.
5. Garnish with slivered almonds before serving.

## Panettone

### Ingredients:

- 3 1/2 cups **flour**
- 1/2 cup **sugar**
- 1 tsp **salt**
- 2 tsp **instant yeast**
- 1/2 cup **milk**
- 3 **eggs**
- 1/2 cup **butter**
- 1 cup **raisins**
- 1/2 cup **candied citrus peel**
- 1 tsp **vanilla extract**

### Instructions:

1. Mix flour, sugar, salt, and yeast.
2. Add milk, eggs, butter, and vanilla to form a dough.
3. Knead the dough until smooth, then let it rise for 2 hours.
4. Add raisins and candied citrus peel.
5. Shape into a loaf, place in a panettone mold, and bake at 350°F (175°C) for 30–40 minutes.

## Colomba Pasquale

**Ingredients:**

- 3 1/2 cups **flour**
- 1/2 cup **sugar**
- 1 tsp **yeast**
- 3 **eggs**
- 1/2 cup **milk**
- 1/2 cup **butter**
- 1/2 tsp **vanilla extract**
- 1/4 cup **candied fruit**
- **Sugar and almonds for topping**

**Instructions:**

1. Mix flour, sugar, and yeast.
2. Add eggs, milk, butter, and vanilla to form a dough.
3. Let the dough rise for 2 hours, then fold in candied fruit.
4. Shape into a dove shape and place on a baking sheet.
5. Top with sugar and almonds, then bake at 350°F (175°C) for 40–50 minutes.

## Ricotta and Pear Tart

### Ingredients:

- **Crust:** 1 1/2 cups **flour**, 1/2 cup **butter**, 1/4 cup **sugar**, 1 **egg**
- **Filling:** 1 cup **ricotta cheese**, 1/2 cup **sugar**, 2 **eggs**, 2 **pears**, peeled and sliced

### Instructions:

1. Preheat the oven to 350°F (175°C).
2. Mix flour, butter, sugar, and egg to form a dough.
3. Roll out dough and line a tart pan.
4. Mix ricotta, sugar, and eggs to form the filling.
5. Pour into the crust and top with pear slices.
6. Bake for 30–35 minutes until set.

## Focaccia Dolce

**Ingredients:**

- 2 1/2 cups **flour**
- 1/4 cup **sugar**
- 1 tsp **instant yeast**
- 1/2 cup **milk**
- 1/4 cup **olive oil**
- 1/2 tsp **salt**
- 1/2 cup **raisins**
- **Powdered sugar for dusting**

**Instructions:**

1. Mix flour, sugar, yeast, and salt.
2. Add milk and olive oil to form a dough, then let rise for 1 hour.
3. Roll the dough out and place in a baking pan.
4. Press raisins into the dough, then let rise for another 30 minutes.
5. Bake at 375°F (190°C) for 20–25 minutes.
6. Dust with powdered sugar before serving.

## Zuppa Inglese

**Ingredients:**

- 1 1/2 cups **sponge cake** (or ladyfingers)
- 1 cup **custard** (pastry cream)
- 1 cup **chocolate custard**
- 1/4 cup **Alchermes** liqueur (or other sweet liqueur)
- **Powdered cocoa for dusting**

**Instructions:**

1. Slice the sponge cake or ladyfingers and soak them in Alchermes liqueur.
2. Layer the soaked cake in a serving dish.
3. Alternate layers of custard and chocolate custard over the cake.
4. Repeat until all ingredients are used.
5. Finish with a dusting of cocoa powder and refrigerate for a few hours before serving.

## Castagnaccio

### Ingredients:

- 2 cups **chestnut flour**
- 1/2 cup **water**
- 2 tbsp **olive oil**
- 1/2 cup **raisins**
- 1/4 cup **pine nuts**
- 1 tbsp **rosemary**, finely chopped
- **Salt** to taste

### Instructions:

1. Preheat the oven to 375°F (190°C).
2. Mix chestnut flour, water, and olive oil to form a smooth batter.
3. Stir in raisins, pine nuts, rosemary, and a pinch of salt.
4. Pour into a greased baking dish and smooth the top.
5. Bake for 30-40 minutes until firm and lightly golden.

## Tortino al Cioccolato

**Ingredients:**

- 1/2 cup **dark chocolate**, chopped
- 1/4 cup **butter**
- 1/2 cup **sugar**
- 2 **eggs**
- 1/4 cup **flour**
- 1/4 tsp **vanilla extract**
- **Powdered sugar** for dusting

**Instructions:**

1. Preheat oven to 425°F (220°C).
2. Melt chocolate and butter together in a heatproof bowl over simmering water.
3. In a separate bowl, beat eggs and sugar until fluffy.
4. Stir the melted chocolate into the egg mixture, then add flour and vanilla.
5. Pour into greased molds and bake for 10–12 minutes until the edges are set but the center is soft.
6. Dust with powdered sugar before serving.

## Sbrisolona

**Ingredients:**

- 2 cups **flour**
- 1 cup **cornmeal**
- 1/2 cup **sugar**
- 1/2 cup **butter**
- 1/2 tsp **baking powder**
- 1/2 cup **chopped almonds**
- 1/4 tsp **vanilla extract**

**Instructions:**

1. Preheat oven to 350°F (175°C).
2. Mix flour, cornmeal, sugar, and baking powder in a bowl.
3. Cut in butter until the mixture resembles coarse crumbs.
4. Stir in almonds and vanilla.
5. Press the dough into a round cake pan, leaving the top crumbly.
6. Bake for 30-35 minutes until golden and crunchy.

## Pasticcini alla Crema

### Ingredients:

- **Puff pastry sheets**
- 1 cup **pastry cream** (custard)
- **Powdered sugar** for dusting

### Instructions:

1. Preheat oven to 375°F (190°C).
2. Cut puff pastry sheets into small squares or circles.
3. Bake pastry for 10-12 minutes until puffed and golden.
4. Fill each pastry with a spoonful of pastry cream.
5. Dust with powdered sugar before serving.

## Focaccia di Recco

### Ingredients:

- 2 cups **flour**
- 1/4 cup **olive oil**
- 1/2 cup **water**
- 1 tsp **salt**
- 1/2 lb **stracchino cheese** (or fresh mozzarella)

### Instructions:

1. Preheat oven to 500°F (260°C).
2. Mix flour, olive oil, water, and salt to form a dough.
3. Roll out dough into thin sheets, then place a layer of cheese between two sheets of dough.
4. Bake on a pizza stone or baking sheet for 10-12 minutes until golden and crispy.

## Ciambellone

### Ingredients:

- 2 cups **flour**
- 1 cup **sugar**
- 1/2 cup **butter**, softened
- 4 **eggs**
- 1/2 cup **milk**
- 1 tsp **baking powder**
- 1 tsp **vanilla extract**
- **Powdered sugar** for dusting

### Instructions:

1. Preheat oven to 350°F (175°C).
2. Cream butter and sugar, then add eggs one at a time.
3. Mix in flour, milk, baking powder, and vanilla.
4. Pour into a greased bundt pan and bake for 40-45 minutes until golden and a toothpick comes out clean.
5. Dust with powdered sugar before serving.

## Frutta Martorana

### Ingredients:

- 2 cups **almond flour**
- 1 1/4 cups **powdered sugar**
- 1 egg white
- **Food coloring** (optional)
- **Honey** for glazing

### Instructions:

1. Mix almond flour, powdered sugar, and egg white to form a dough.
2. Shape the dough into fruits (apples, pears, oranges, etc.).
3. Use food coloring to paint the fruits to resemble real ones.
4. Brush with honey for a glossy finish and let them set.

www.ingramcontent.com/pod-product-compliance
Lightning Source LLC
LaVergne TN
LVHW081505060526
838201LV00056BA/2949